KENNY JOHNSON

The Power of a Praying Man

KLP

KINGDOM LEGACY
PRESS

To God, my Source, my Strength, and my Shepherd—thank You for calling me, refining me, and using me for Your glory.

To my wife, my greatest blessing and partner in purpose—thank you for your love, faith, and constant support. You are my answered prayer.

To my children—may this book be a light for your path, a guide for your purpose, and a reminder that your identity is found in Christ alone.

This is more than a book.
This is our legacy.
All glory to God.

Contents

Preface

The Sacred Name: Yahshua (Jesus)

Throughout this book, you will notice the name Yahshua (Jesus) used consistently in every prayer, scripture, and spiritual reference. This is not by accident. It is a divine restoration—an invitation to deeper understanding and reverence for the One who came to save.

1. Yahshua: The Original Name of the Messiah

Before Greek, Latin, or English translations existed, the Son of God was called by His Hebrew name: Yahshua (י ה ש ו ע), meaning "Yah is salvation" or "Yahweh saves." This name embodies His mission and identity—not only as Savior but as the fulfillment of the Father's promise.

"She will give birth to a son, and you are to give Him the name Yahshua, because He will save His people from their sins."
  (Matthew 1:21, Hebrew Roots Translation)

In most Bibles, this verse uses the name Jesus, but in the original tongue, Yahshua was the name given. His name connects to the divine name of the Father—Yahweh—revealing the unity between Father and Son.

"I have come in My Father's name, and you do not receive Me."
  (John 5:43)

"Your name, O YHWH, endures forever, Your renown, O YHWH, through all generations."
  (Psalm 135:13)

The very name Yahshua carries that same eternal Name—Yah—which is lost in the Greek and English forms.

2. *Jesus: The Translated Name with Continued Grace*

The name "Jesus" came into popular usage through a series of linguistic transitions:

Hebrew "Yahshua"

Greek "Iēsous" (Greek lacks the "Y" and "sh" sounds)

Latin "Iesus"

English "Jesus" (with the letter "J" being introduced around the 16th century)

Although the name "Jesus" is not linguistically the same as "Yahshua," it carries spiritual power because of the faith and reverence placed in it by generations of believers. God responds to the heart, not merely phonetics.

"There is no other name under heaven given among men by which we must be saved."

(Acts 4:12)

"For whoever calls on the name of the Lord shall be saved."
   (Romans 10:13)

These verses affirm the saving power of the name, even when pronounced differently, so long as the heart is aligned in truth and faith.

3. Reclaiming the Power of the Name

In these last days, the Father is restoring lost truths—identities, cultures, and languages that were stripped through colonization, translation, and assimilation. Reclaiming the name Yahshua is not to dismiss or diminish the name "Jesus," but to honor the original and reveal the fullness of His identity.

"The name of YHWH is a strong tower; the righteous run to it and are safe."
   (Proverbs 18:10)

"Then I will restore to the peoples a pure language, that they all may call on the name of YHWH, to serve Him with one accord."
   (Zephaniah 3:9)

The enemy has always sought to distort identity and language, because names carry power, assignment, and spiritual authority. The restoration of Yahshua's name is part of the greater awakening happening among God's people.

4. How This Book Will Use His Name

To walk in both truth and accessibility, this book will use Yahshua (Jesus) throughout—bridging the gap between what has been passed down and what is being restored.

"Yahshua the Messiah is the same yesterday, today, and forever."
  (Hebrews 13:8, Hebrew Roots Bible)

Every prayer, every scripture, and every reflection is written to honor both the faith many were raised with and the deeper truth now being revealed. Let this understanding open your spirit to greater revelation. May you call on Him, not out of tradition, but with truth and intimacy. Whether you say Jesus or Yahshua, may your prayers be filled with power, and your walk be filled with light.

"And you shall know the truth, and the truth shall make you free."
  (John 8:32)

Introduction

The Journey of a Praying Man

Growing up in a Christian household, I was always taught the importance of prayer. My family would begin and end each day in prayer together, setting the foundation for what I believed was a strong spiritual life. But like many men, as I grew older, went to college, and pursued my own desires, my prayer life dwindled. I became focused on what I wanted for myself, rather than what God wanted for me. I didn't realize it at the time, but my lack of prayer was disconnecting me from God's guidance, wisdom, and favor. "Never stop praying." – 1 Thessalonians 5:17 (NLT)

A Defining Moment – The Book That Changed Everything

On September 8, 2024, my wedding day, my wife and I received a gift that would change our lives forever. Our mentors, Pastor James and Heather Burks, gifted us two books: The Power of a Praying Husband & The Power of a Praying Wife by Stormie Omartian. At first, we thanked them but didn't open the books immediately. It wasn't until about a month later, when we found ourselves struggling to connect deeply as husband and wife, that God led us back to them.

Realizing I Had It Backwards

As the head of my household, I knew my responsibility as a husband was great, but I didn't fully understand how prayer played a role in leading my wife and family. I was frustrated in my marriage, feeling like I wasn't getting through to my wife, yet I had never stopped to ask: Am I truly leading spiritually? Am I requiring my wife to submit before I submit to God? When I opened The Power of a Praying Husband, the very first chapter convicted me. I had it all backwards. "For a husband is the head of his wife as Christ is the head of the church. He is the Savior of his body, the church." – Ephesians 5:23 (NLT) I realized that I couldn't expect my wife to follow me if I wasn't first following God. Through prayer, repentance, and surrender, I began to pray for my wife, for my marriage, and for myself as a husband. And something powerful happened.

The Breakthrough – The Power of Praying for Others

As I prayed more for my wife, I saw real change—not just in her, but in me. Our communication improved. We had more patience, grace, and love for each other. God began aligning our hearts. I was so impacted that I started praying for my children, my family, my finances, my purpose, and even strangers. The more I prayed, the more I saw God move. "The earnest prayer of a righteous person has great power and produces wonderful results." – James 5:16 (NLT)

The Missing Book – A Call from God

As my prayer life grew, I began gifting copies of The Power of a

Praying Husband and other Stormie Omartian books to friends, family, and clients.

The Power of a Praying Parent

The Power of a Praying Teen

The Power of Praying for Your Adult Children

The Power of a Praying Grandparent

The Power of a Praying Woman

The Power of a Praying Wife

The Power of a Praying Husband

Then one day, I noticed something missing. There was no book called The Power of a Praying Man. I immediately felt in my spirit that this needed to exist. At first, I thought, Someone else should write it. But time and time again, God confirmed to me—through people, messages, and divine signs— I was called to write this book. "For God is working in you, giving you the desire and the power to do what pleases him." – Philippians 2:13 (NLT)

Why This Book? Why Now?

Men today are facing spiritual battles like never before. Distractions are everywhere. Mental health struggles are rising. Fathers and leaders are being removed from homes. Men are losing their sense of purpose. The enemy wants to keep men from praying, because he knows that when a man prays, his: Marriage is strengthened. Children are protected. Finances are blessed. Purpose is revealed. This book is a call to action for every man to rise up, reclaim his spiritual authority, and walk in boldness, faith, and power. "Be on guard. Stand firm in the faith. Be courageous. Be strong." – 1 Corinthians 16:13 (NLT)

What You Will Learn in This Book

In The Power of a Praying Man, you will learn:
   How to build a strong prayer life
   How to pray for yourself, your wife, and your children
   How to break generational curses and create generational blessings
   How prayer, affirmations, journalism, and meditation work together
   How to overcome fear, anxiety, and negative thoughts
   How to use fasting and prayer for breakthrough

This book is not just about knowledge—it is about transformation.

Each chapter will include:
   Biblical principles and scripture-based prayers
   Personal testimonies and real-life applications
   Scientific studies on the power of prayer and affirmations
   Challenges and exercises to apply what you learn

"Faith by itself isn't enough. Unless it produces good deeds, it is dead and useless." – James 2:17 (NLT)

A Final Word Before We Begin

If you are reading this book, it is not by accident. God has called you here for a reason. This is not just a book—it's an invitation to transformation. It's time for men to rise up in prayer, walk in their God-given authority, and claim victory in every area of their lives.

4

A Prayer of Dedication

Father, I dedicate this book to You. May every man who reads it be transformed, strengthened, and renewed in prayer. Let this book serve as a tool to restore families, heal marriages, and awaken men to their true purpose. Let every word be guided by Your Holy Spirit, and let every heart be open to receive Your truth. I surrender this book, this mission, and this calling to You. In (Yahshua's) Jesus' name, Amen.

1

Chapter 1: Why Men Must Pray

The Spiritual Battle Against Men's Prayer Lives

If there is one thing Satan fears, it's a man in prayer. From the beginning of time, the enemy has tried to separate men from God—because he knows that when a man walks in alignment with the Lord, he: Leads his family with wisdom and authority. Walks in provision and purpose. Has peace, strength, and discipline. But the moment a man stops praying, he becomes vulnerable. His mind is clouded with doubt and fear. His heart is hardened with pride and anger. His purpose feels distant and unclear. This is why so many men today feel lost, anxious, and unfulfilled—because the enemy has distracted them from their connection to God. "Put on all of God's armor so that you will be able to stand firm against all strategies of the devil." – Ephesians 6:11 (NLT)

The First Attack in Any War – Communication

My father, a veteran of Operation Iraqi Freedom, once taught me something about war: The first strategy in any battle is to disrupt the enemy's communication. If soldiers can't receive instructions, they become confused, uncoordinated, and weak. This makes them easy to defeat. That's exactly what Satan is doing to men today—he's cutting off our spiritual communication with God. He fills our schedules with busyness so we feel like we have no time to pray. He tempts us with distractions, entertainment, and social media to keep us spiritually dull. He fills our minds with self-doubt, guilt, and condemnation, making us feel unworthy to talk to God. But here's the truth: You don't have to be perfect to pray. You don't have to have it all together to pray. You just have to be willing to talk to your Father. "Come close to God, and God will come close to you." – James 4:8 (NLT)

Prayer is the Key to Everything You Desire

Every man wants: Clarity on his purpose. Peace in his mind. Strength in his body. Provision for his family. And every one of these things begins with prayer. "And we are confident that he hears us whenever we ask for anything that pleases him." – 1 John 5:14 (NLT) When a man prays first, everything else falls into place. Your marriage strengthens. Your finances align. Your mental health improves. Your purpose becomes clear. That's because prayer is not just talking—it's transformation. "The Lord is close to all who call on him, yes, to all who call on him in truth." – Psalm 145:18 (NLT)

The Cost of a Prayerless Life

A man who doesn't pray lives a life of constant struggle. He relies

7

on his own strength instead of God's. He is easily discouraged and distracted. He feels lost, empty, and unfulfilled. Even great men in the Bible struggled when they didn't seek God. King Saul – Lost his throne because he stopped seeking God's wisdom (1 Samuel 28:6-7). Samson – Was led by his own desires and lost his strength (Judges 16:20). Adam – Failed to intercede for his wife, leading to the fall of mankind (Genesis 3:6-7). Without prayer, men are left exposed to the enemy's attacks. But when a man prays, he is covered. "For the Lord protects the bones of the righteous; not one of them is broken!" – Psalm 34:20 (NLT)

Yahshua (Jesus) – The Ultimate Example of a Praying Man

Yahshua (Jesus) was the Son of God, yet He still prioritized prayer above all things. Before choosing His disciples, He spent all night in prayer (Luke 6:12). Before performing miracles, He prayed (John 11:41-42). Before facing the cross, He prayed with such intensity that He sweat blood (Luke 22:44). If Yahshua (Jesus) needed prayer, how much more do we? "But Yahshua (Jesus) often withdrew to the wilderness for prayer." – Luke 5:16 (NLT) A praying man is a protected man, a wise man, and a strong man.

A 7-Day Prayer Challenge to Strengthen Your Connection with God

For the next 7 days, commit to:

1. Setting aside 10 minutes every morning to pray
2. Keeping a journal of your prayers and reflections
3. Praying before making any major decisions
4. Speaking to God throughout the day, like you would a

trusted friend

"Don't worry about anything; instead, pray about everything."
– Philippians 4:6 (NLT)

A Prayer for Strength in Your Prayer Life

Father, I come before You as a man who desires to grow in prayer. Forgive me for the times I have relied on my own strength instead of seeking You first. Your Word says in Matthew 6:33 that when I seek You first, everything I need will be provided. Teach me to be a man of prayer, to put You first, and to walk in Your wisdom and power. In Yahshua's (Jesus') name, Amen.

Key Takeaways

1. A man in prayer is a man in power.
2. Satan's first attack is cutting off communication between men and God.
3. Without prayer, men live in confusion, frustration, and weakness.
4. Yahshua (Jesus) showed us that a strong prayer life is the key to everything.

The next 7 days are your opportunity to rebuild your prayer life.

"Be strong and courageous! Do not be afraid or discouraged. For the Lord your God is with you wherever you go." – Joshua 1:9 (NLT)

Chapter 2: Praying for Yourself – Strength, Discipline, and Wisdom

Why Praying for Yourself is Not Selfish—It's Necessary

Many men struggle with the idea of praying for themselves. Some feel unworthy, thinking they must be perfect before coming to God. Others believe it's selfish, feeling they should pray only for others. Some assume God is too busy to care about their personal needs. But the truth is—if you don't pray for yourself, you will not have the strength to pray for anyone else. Yahshua (Jesus) Himself prayed for His own strength and wisdom before taking on His mission. "He went on a little farther and bowed with his face to the ground, praying, 'My Father! If it is possible, let this cup of suffering be taken away from me. Yet I want Your will to be done, not mine.'" – Matthew 26:39 (NLT) If Yahshua (Jesus) prayed for Himself, then we should too. Praying for strength, discipline, and wisdom is not selfish—it is necessary for a man to walk in his purpose.

The Five-Finger Prayer Method – Covering Every Area of Life

On the way to a work-related conference, my wife and I listened to a sermon online about prayer. The pastor shared a simple but powerful method called the Five-Finger Prayer—a way to ensure we pray for every key area of life.

The Five-Finger Prayer Method

1. Thumb – Pray for Your Family:
   This is the closest finger to your heart. Pray for your wife, children, parents, and loved ones.

2. Index Finger – Pray for Leaders:
   This finger points forward, symbolizing direction. Pray for pastors, mentors, government leaders, and those who guide others.

3. Middle Finger – Pray for Influencers:
   This is the tallest finger, representing those with influence. Pray for business owners, celebrities, athletes, and culture leaders to use their platform for good.

4. Ring Finger – Pray for the Weak and Needy:
   The ring finger is the weakest—pray for the homeless, widows, orphans, and those in need of healing.

5. Pinky Finger – Pray for Yourself:
   The smallest finger reminds us of humility—yet it is still necessary. Pray for strength, wisdom, and protection.

By following this method, we ensure our prayers are balanced— covering ourselves, our families, and the world around us.

"The Lord gives wisdom; from His mouth come knowledge and understanding." – Proverbs 2:6 (NLT)

Praying for Strength – Overcoming Life's Pressures

Every man will face challenges, temptations, and trials—but God never intended for us to face them alone. When you pray for strength, you are asking God to: Help you endure hardships without breaking. Give you resilience in temptation. Provide endurance in your responsibilities. "I can do everything through Christ, who gives me strength." – Philippians 4:13 (NLT)

Praying for Discipline – Building a Strong Foundation

Discipline is the key to every great achievement in life—spiritually, physically, financially, and mentally. A disciplined man prays even when he doesn't feel like it. A disciplined man stays committed to his goals and purpose. A disciplined man resists distractions and temptations. Without discipline, a man is easily shaken. "A person without self-control is like a city with broken-down walls." – Proverbs 25:28 (NLT)

When you pray for discipline, you are asking God to:
Give you self-control in your actions and emotions
Help you overcome procrastination and laziness
Strengthen your daily habits in prayer, health, and productivity
Praying for Wisdom – Making the Right Decisions

Men are constantly faced with decisions that shape their future—who to marry, where to work, how to lead. A wise man doesn't rush into decisions—he seeks God first. King Solomon, the wisest man in history, did not ask for money, power, or success—he asked for wisdom. "Give me an understanding heart so that I can govern your people well and know the difference between right and wrong. For who by himself is able to govern this great people of Yours?" – 1 Kings 3:9 (NLT) God was so pleased with this request that He gave Solomon not only wisdom—but also wealth, influence, and success. "Seek His will in all you do, and He will show you which path to take." – Proverbs 3:6 (NLT)

When you pray for wisdom, you are asking God to:
    Guide you in your decisions
    Give you discernment between good and bad influences
    Help you make choices that align with His plan

The PRAY Method – A Simple Framework for Daily Prayer

To make prayer a consistent habit, I created a simple acronym:
    P – Pray to the Father (Start by thanking God and acknowledging His greatness.)
    R – Read the Word (Meditate on a Bible verse related to your needs.)
    A – Apply the Lesson (Ask yourself, "How can I live out this scripture today?")
    Y – Yield to God (Surrender control and trust God's plan for your life.)

This method ensures prayer is not just a routine, but a powerful daily transformation. "Devote yourselves to prayer with an alert mind and a thankful heart." – Colossians 4:2 (NLT)

A 7-Day Challenge for Strength, Discipline, and Wisdom

For the next 7 days, commit to:

1. Praying each morning for personal strength and discipline
2. Using the Five-Finger Prayer Method
3. Journaling your daily prayers and reflections
4. Applying the PRAY method to stay spiritually disciplined

"If you need wisdom, ask our generous God, and He will give it to you. He will not rebuke you for asking." – James 1:5 (NLT)

A Prayer for Strength, Discipline, and Wisdom

Father, I thank You for the strength You provide each day. I ask for discipline to stay faithful in prayer, to resist distractions, and to live a life that honors You. Fill me with wisdom, so I may make decisions that align with Your will. Your Word says in James 1:5 that if I need wisdom, I only need to ask, and You will give it freely. I receive Your strength, discipline, and wisdom today. In Yahshua's (Jesus') name, Amen.

Key Takeaways

1. A man must pray for himself to remain strong in his faith and leadership.
2. The Five-Finger Prayer Method helps cover all areas of life.
3. Strength, discipline, and wisdom are key for a man's success.
4. The PRAY method ensures a consistent and effective prayer life.

5. Daily prayer leads to daily victories.

"The Lord gives His people strength. The Lord blesses them with peace." – Psalm 29:11 (NLT)

3

Chapter 3: Praying for Your Wife – Covering Her in the Spirit

Why Every Husband Must Pray for His Wife

A husband is called to be the spiritual covering of his wife, just as Christ is the covering of the church. This means you are responsible for interceding for her. This means you must pray for her protection, wisdom, and strength. This means you are called to love her as Christ loved the church—which includes praying for her daily. "For a husband is the head of his wife as Christ is the head of the church. He is the Savior of his body, the church." – Ephesians 5:23 (NLT) One of the greatest acts of love you can offer your wife is consistent and intentional prayer on her behalf.

Praying for the Wife God Has for You (For Single Men)

If you are not yet married, this chapter still applies to you. Pray for the wife God is preparing for you. Pray that God prepares you to be a godly husband. Pray for wisdom in choosing a life partner.

"The man who finds a wife finds a treasure, and he receives favor from the Lord." – Proverbs 18:22 (NLT) Many men rush into relationships based on physical attraction, emotions, or convenience, rather than seeking God's wisdom and direction. As a single man, pray: That you grow in spiritual maturity before marriage. That your future wife is protected and strengthened wherever she is. That you align with a woman who seeks after God first. If you trust God with your finances and career, why wouldn't you trust Him with choosing your wife? "A prudent wife is a gift from the Lord." – Proverbs 19:14 (NLT)

The Role of a Praying Husband

A praying husband invites God's presence into his marriage. He covers his wife in prayer to protect her spiritually and emotionally. He prays for her mind, body, and spirit to align with God's will. He intercedes for her dreams, struggles, and personal growth. A wife who is prayed over feels loved, valued, and covered. When you pray for your wife, you: Strengthen your marriage bond. Build a foundation of trust and unity. Invite God's favor into your relationship. "Let each one of you love his wife as himself, and let the wife see that she respects her husband." – Ephesians 5:33 (NLT)

What Should You Pray Over Your Wife?

1. Pray for Her Spiritual Growth:
   Ask God to increase her faith, wisdom, and discernment. "I pray that from His glorious, unlimited resources He will em-power you with inner strength through His Spirit." – Ephesians 3:16 (NLT)

17

2. Pray for Her Protection:

Cover her in God's hedge of protection against spiritual and physical harm. "The Lord Himself watches over you! The Lord stands beside you as your protective shade." – Psalm 121:5 (NLT)

3. Pray for Her Emotional Well-being:

Women carry many burdens—pray that she finds peace and rest in God. "Give all your worries and cares to God, for He cares about you." – 1 Peter 5:7 (NLT)

4. Pray for Her Strength and Endurance:

Ask God to give her strength in all that she does—at work, at home, and in life. "She is clothed with strength and dignity, and she laughs without fear of the future." – Proverbs 31:25 (NLT)

5. Pray for Her Purpose and Calling:

Your wife was created with a divine purpose—pray that she walks boldly in it. "For we are God's masterpiece. He has created us anew in Christ Yahshua (Jesus), so we can do the good things He planned for us long ago." – Ephesians 2:10 (NLT)

6. Pray for Your Marriage:

Ask God to protect and strengthen your marriage, keeping it pure, joyful, and Christ-centered. "Let no one split apart what God has joined together." – Mark 10:9 (NLT)

The Power of a Husband's Blessing

One of the most powerful things you can do as a husband is to speak blessings over your wife. Lay hands on her and pray over her. Speak life, love, and prosperity into your marriage. Remind her who she is in Christ. Your words carry power—use them to build her up and strengthen your relationship. "The tongue can bring death or life; those who love to talk will reap the consequences." – Proverbs 18:21 (NLT)A 7-Day Challenge: Praying for Your Wife

For the next 7 days, commit to:

1. Praying for your wife (or future wife) every morning and night
2. Speaking words of encouragement and blessing over her
3. Asking her how you can pray for her specific needs
4. Watch how God moves in your marriage when you cover your wife in prayer.

"The Lord bless you and keep you; the Lord make His face shine on you and be gracious to you." – Numbers 6:24-25 (NLT)

A Prayer for Your Wife

Father, I thank You for the gift of my wife. I lift her up to You today, asking that You strengthen her, guide her, and fill her with peace. Protect her heart and mind from anxiety and fear, and help her walk in confidence and joy. Your Word says in Psalm 121:5 that You are our protector—let Your presence be her covering. Bless our marriage, deepen our love, and align our hearts with Yours. In Yahshua's (Jesus') name, Amen.

Key Takeaways

1. A husband's greatest responsibility is to cover his wife in prayer.
2. Single men should pray for the wife God has for them.
3. A man who prays for his wife strengthens their marriage.
4. Pray for your wife's protection, wisdom, emotional well-being, and purpose.
5. Speaking blessings over your wife builds her faith and confidence.

"Husbands, love your wives, just as Christ loved the church. He gave up His life for her." – Ephesians 5:25 (NLT)

4

Chapter 4: Praying for Your Children – Raising Kingdom Leaders

The Role of a Father in Raising Kingdom Leaders

As a father, your greatest responsibility is to lead your children in the ways of the Lord. You are their protector. You are their provider. You are their spiritual covering. But above all—you are their first example of a godly man. Your children will learn how to pray, how to trust God, and how to lead by watching you. "Direct your children onto the right path, and when they are older, they will not leave it." – Proverbs 22:6 (NLT)

Why Prayer is the Greatest Gift You Can Give Your Children

Your prayers shape their future. Your prayers protect them from harm. Your prayers release blessings over their lives. A father's prayers never expire—they continue working long after he is gone. Many men leave behind money and possessions for their children—but a legacy of prayer is far more valuable. "The godly walk with integrity; blessed are their children who follow them."

– Proverbs 20:7 (NLT)

What to Pray Over Your Children

1. Pray for Their Protection:
Ask God to guard their hearts, minds, and bodies from harm. "The Lord Himself watches over you! The Lord stands beside you as your protective shade." – Psalm 121:5 (NLT)

2. Pray for Their Identity in Christ:
Declare that your children will know who they are in God and not be deceived by the world. "For we are God's masterpiece. He has created us anew in Christ Yahshua (Jesus)." – Ephesians 2:10 (NLT)

3. Pray for Their Friendships and Relationships:
Ask God to surround them with godly influences and remove toxic people from their lives. "Walk with the wise and become wise; associate with fools and get in trouble." – Proverbs 13:20 (NLT)

4. Pray for Their Purpose and Calling:
Declare that your children will discover and fulfill their God-given destiny. "For I know the plans I have for you, says the Lord. They are plans for good and not for disaster, to give you a future and a hope." – Jeremiah 29:11 (NLT)

5. Pray for Their Obedience and Wisdom:
Ask God to give them discernment and a heart that seeks after Him. "Fear of the Lord is the foundation of true knowledge, but fools despise wisdom and discipline." – Proverbs 1:7 (NLT)

Leading by Example – Your Children Imitate What They See

Your children will not just listen to what you say—they will imitate what you do. If they see you pray, they will learn to pray. If they see you seek God, they will seek Him too. If they see you walk in faith, they will believe God for themselves. "Follow my example, as I follow the example of Christ." – 1 Corinthians 11:1 (NLT) If you want to raise godly children, you must first be a godly man.

A Father's Blessing – Speaking Life Over Your Children

Your words carry power—speak life, purpose, and blessings over your children daily. Lay hands on them and pray for them. Tell them who they are in Christ. Declare God's promises over their future. "The tongue can bring death or life; those who love to talk will reap the consequences." – Proverbs 18:21 (NLT) Instead of saying, "You're never going to change." "You always mess things up." "You'll never be successful." Say, "You are a child of God, created for greatness." "God has a plan for your life." "You will be a leader and a blessing to others."

A 7-Day Challenge: Praying for Your Children

For the next 7 days, commit to:

1. Praying over your children every morning and night.
2. Speaking life over them through words of affirmation.
3. Praying for their protection, identity, and future.
4. Leading by example—letting them see you pray and seek God.

5. Watch how God moves in their lives as you cover them in prayer.

"The Lord bless you and keep you; the Lord make His face shine on you and be gracious to you." – Numbers 6:24-25 (NLT)

A Prayer for Your Children

Father, I lift my children up to You today. I ask for Your protection over their hearts, minds, and bodies. Let them grow in wisdom, favor, and strength. Surround them with godly influences and keep them from harm. Your Word says in Jeremiah 29:11 that You have a plan for their future. Let them walk in that plan and fulfill their divine purpose. In Yahshua's (Jesus') name, Amen.

Key Takeaways

1. A father's greatest responsibility is to cover his children in prayer.
2. Prayer shapes their identity, protection, and purpose.
3. Your children will imitate your faith—lead by example.
4. Your words have power—speak life over your children.
5. Praying fathers raise strong, godly children.

"As for me and my family, we will serve the Lord." – Joshua 24:15 (NLT)

5

Chapter 5: Praying for Financial Prosperity and Generational Wealth

Why Men Must Pray Over Their Finances

Finances are a critical area of a man's life: God calls men to be providers (1 Timothy 5:8). Money is a tool, not a master (Matthew 6:24). Financial stewardship is part of our responsibility (Luke 16:10-11). However, many men experience stress, lack, and frustration in their finances because they try to manage them without seeking God first. The world teaches that wealth comes through hustle, grinding, and self-reliance—but God's way is different. When you put God first in your finances, He will order your steps to financial prosperity. "Seek the Kingdom of God above all else, and live righteously, and He will give you everything you need." – Matthew 6:33 (NLT)

Faith Without Works is Dead – Taking Action in Finances

Many men pray for financial breakthrough but don't take the right actions. They want debt freedom but continue to overspend. They want wealth but refuse to develop financial wisdom. They ask for opportunities but don't prepare to receive them. "Just as the body is dead without breath, so also faith is dead without good works." – James 2:26 (NLT) God calls men to both pray and act. Pray for financial wisdom – then learn how to manage money. Pray for opportunities – then position yourself for success. Pray for increase – then be faithful with what you already have.

The Purpose of Financial Prosperity – Generational Wealth

Money is not about status or personal gain—it is about stewardship and legacy. God blesses you so you can bless others (2 Corinthians 9:8). Wealth is a tool to advance God's Kingdom (Proverbs 11:25). Your financial decisions affect your children and future generations. A man who does not think about generational wealth is living short-sighted. "Good people leave an inheritance to their grandchildren, but the sinner's wealth passes to the godly." – Proverbs 13:22 (NLT)

Tithing – Honoring God with Your Wealth

One of the most powerful financial principles in the Bible is tithing—giving the first 10% of your income to God. Many men hesitate to tithe, thinking they can't afford it. But in reality, you can't afford NOT to tithe. Tithing invites God's protection over your finances. Tithing removes the curse of lack. Tithing opens the door for financial blessings. "Bring all the tithes into the storehouse so there will be enough food in my Temple. If you do," says the Lord of Heaven's Armies, "I will open the windows of heaven for you. I will pour out a blessing so great you won't have enough room to take it in." – Malachi 3:10 (NLT) Tithing is not about giving God money—it's about trusting Him as your Provider.

What to Pray Over Your Finances

1. Pray for Wisdom in Financial Decisions:
   Ask God to give you discernment in how to earn, spend, and invest. "If you need wisdom, ask our generous God, and He will give it to you." – James 1:5 (NLT)

2. Pray for Debt Freedom and Financial Breakthrough:
   Ask God to help you break free from financial burdens and move toward abundance. "The borrower is servant to the lender." – Proverbs 22:7 (NLT)

3. Pray for Opportunities and Divine Connections:
   Ask God to open doors for business, investments, and career growth. "Commit your actions to the Lord, and your plans will succeed." – Proverbs 16:3 (NLT)

4. Pray for Generational Wealth:
   Declare that your finances will not just provide for you, but for your children's children. "The Lord will send a blessing on your barns and on everything you put your hand to." – Deuteronomy 28:8 (NLT)

A 7-Day Financial Prayer Challenge

For the next 7 days, commit to:

1. Praying daily over your finances, debt, and wealth-building strategies.
2. Tithing or sowing into a ministry or cause.
3. Eliminating wasteful spending and creating a financial plan.
4. Declaring financial increase and favor over your life.
5. Watch how God shifts your financial situation as you seek Him first.

"The blessing of the Lord makes a person rich, and He adds no sorrow with it." – Proverbs 10:22 (NLT)

A Prayer for Financial Prosperity and Generational Wealth

Father, I come before You as my Provider. I trust You with my finances, and I surrender my financial struggles to You. Your Word says in Malachi 3:10 that if I honor You with my wealth, You will open the windows of heaven over my life. I ask for wisdom in managing money, for divine opportunities, and for a mindset of abundance. Let my finances be a testimony of Your faithfulness, and may I build a legacy that honors You. In Yahshua's (Jesus') name, Amen.

Key Takeaways

1. Financial prosperity comes from seeking God first.
2. Faith without works is dead—prayer must be followed by financial discipline.
3. Generational wealth is a biblical principle.
4. Tithing opens the door for financial increase.
5. Your financial breakthrough starts with prayer and action.

"Honor the Lord with your wealth and with the best part of everything you produce." – Proverbs 3:9 (NLT)

6

Chapter 6: Praying for Your Purpose and Calling

Discovering Your God-Given Purpose

Every man has asked at some point in his life: What am I supposed to do? Why am I here? What is my purpose? The answer is simple: Your purpose is to serve God and fulfill the mission He has assigned to you. However, finding that purpose requires seeking Him in prayer. "For we are God's masterpiece. He has created us anew in Christ Yahshua (Jesus), so we can do the good things He planned for us long ago." – Ephesians 2:10 (NLT) When you align with God's purpose, you experience: Peace – Knowing you're on the right path. Provision – God supplying your every need. Power – Walking in divine authority. But when you resist His calling, life feels: Confusing – You feel lost and directionless. Frustrating – You struggle without progress. Empty – No amount of success satisfies. "Seek His will in all you do, and He will show you which path to take." – Proverbs 3:6 (NLT)

God Expands Your Purpose When You Submit to Him

Shortly after my enlightenment in Christ, I realized that men often create their own purpose—chasing money, status, and worldly success. But when we align with God's purpose, He expands our vision beyond what we ever imagined. Moses thought his purpose was to be a shepherd—but God called him to lead a nation (Exodus 3:10). Paul thought his purpose was to enforce the law—but God called him to spread the Gospel (Acts 9:15). Peter thought his purpose was to catch fish—but Yahshua (Jesus) called him to catch souls (Matthew 4:19). If you're unsure of your purpose, start by seeking God in prayer. "You can make many plans, but the Lord's purpose will prevail." – Proverbs 19:21 (NLT)

When You Don't Know What to Pray, the Spirit Intercedes

There were moments in my life when I didn't even know how to pray about my purpose. But I learned that the Holy Spirit intercedes on our behalf. "And the Holy Spirit helps us in our weakness. For example, we don't know what God wants us to pray for. But the Holy Spirit prays for us with groanings that cannot be expressed in words." – Romans 8:26 (NLT) If you feel stuck, ask God: "Lord, what have You created me for?" "How can I serve You with my talents?" "What steps should I take next?" He will answer in His perfect timing.

Biblical Men Who Prayed for Direction

1. Solomon – Prayed for Wisdom Before Leading:
   Instead of praying for money or success, Solomon asked God

31

for wisdom—and received both wisdom and wealth. "Give me an understanding heart so that I can govern Your people well and know the difference between right and wrong." – 1 Kings 3:9 (NLT)

2. Moses – Prayed for Guidance:

Moses didn't feel qualified to lead Israel, but when he prayed for direction, God showed him the way. "If You don't personally go with us, don't make us leave this place." – Exodus 33:15 (NLT)

3. Yahshua (Jesus) – Prayed Before Making Major Decisions:

Before choosing His disciples, Yahshua (Jesus) spent all night in prayer. "One day soon afterward, Yahshua (Jesus) went up on a mountain to pray, and He prayed to God all night." – Luke 6:12 (NLT) If Yahshua (Jesus) needed to pray for direction, how much more do we?

How Prayer Shapes Your Mindset and Destiny

Science confirms what the Bible already teaches: Affirmations and prayer rewire the brain. Neuroplasticity shows that thoughts shape reality. Repeated prayers and declarations strengthen faith. Every time you pray, you: Train your mind to trust in God. Strengthen your spiritual authority. Develop a faith-driven mindset. "Faith shows the reality of what we hope for; it is the evidence of things we cannot see." – Hebrews 11:1 (NLT)

A 7-Day Purpose Prayer Challenge

For the next 7 days, commit to:

1. Praying for clarity about your calling.
2. Asking God to open the right doors and close the wrong ones.
3. Declaring scriptures over your life.
4. Listening for God's direction and journaling what you hear.

"If you remain in Me and My words remain in you, you may ask for anything you want, and it will be granted!" – John 15:7 (NLT)

A Prayer for Purpose and Calling

Father, I seek You today, asking for wisdom and clarity in my purpose. Your Word says in Proverbs 3:6 that when I seek You, You will direct my steps. I surrender my plans and ask that You reveal the path You have set for me. Remove any distractions or fears that keep me from walking boldly in my calling. Let me be a light in my workplace, my home, and my community. Align my desires with Yours, and expand my vision to serve You fully. In Yahshua's (Jesus') name, Amen.

Key Takeaways

1. Your purpose is found in seeking God, not chasing success.
2. When you submit to God's plan, He expands your vision.
3. The Holy Spirit intercedes when you don't know what to pray.
4. Biblical men like Solomon, Moses, and Yahshua (Jesus) prayed before major decisions.
5. Prayer reprograms the mind to align with God's will.

"For God is working in you, giving you the desire and the power to do what pleases Him." – Philippians 2:13 (NLT)

7

Chapter 7: Praying for Your Mind – Overcoming Fear, Anxiety, and Negative Thoughts

The Mind is the Battlefield

The greatest battles a man will ever face are not fought with his fists—they are fought in his mind. Fear tells you that you're not enough. Anxiety makes you worry about things you can't control. Negative thoughts convince you that you'll never change. This is exactly how Satan operates—he attacks men by planting seeds of doubt, fear, and insecurity in their minds. "For God has not given us a spirit of fear and timidity, but of power, love, and self-discipline." – 2 Timothy 1:7 (NLT) If the enemy can control your thoughts, he can weaken your faith, steal your confidence, and keep you from fulfilling your purpose.

Even Yahshua's (Jesus') Mind Was Attacked by Satan

Satan knows the power of the mind—that's why he even tried

to manipulate Yahshua's (Jesus') thoughts. During Yahshua's (Jesus') 40 days of fasting, Satan tempted Him with fear, doubt, and false promises: "Turn these stones into bread." (Doubt God's provision). "Throw Yourself down." (Test God's protection). "Bow down to me." (Compromise for success). "Then Yahshua (Jesus) was led by the Spirit into the wilderness to be tempted there by the devil." – Matthew 4:1 (NLT) But Yahshua (Jesus) fought back with the Word of God—showing us that the only way to defeat Satan's lies is with truth and prayer.

Your Thoughts Shape Your Reality

Science confirms what God's Word has always said—your thoughts create the foundation for your life. The average person has 60,000 thoughts per day. Over 80% of those thoughts are negative. Your brain is wired to repeat what you consistently think. "For as he thinks in his heart, so is he." – Proverbs 23:7 (NLT) This means: If you constantly think about failure, you will struggle. If you constantly think about stress, you will feel anxious. If you constantly think about God's promises, you will walk in victory. This is why prayer is essential—it rewires your mind to align with God's truth.

The Enemy's Top Lies vs. God's Truth

The devil whispers lies to keep you weak. But when you pray and declare God's truth, you break free. By replacing negative thoughts with scripture, you renew your mind and take back control. "Do not be conformed to this world, but be transformed by the renewing of your mind." – Romans 12:2 (NLT)

What to Pray Over Your Mind

1. Pray for Peace and a Sound Mind:
Ask God to remove worry, stress, and fear and fill you with His peace. "Don't worry about anything; instead, pray about everything." – Philippians 4:6 (NLT)

2. Pray for Strength to Resist Temptation:
Ask God to give you the strength to shut down negative thoughts before they take root. "We take captive every thought to make it obedient to Christ." – 2 Corinthians 10:5 (NLT)

3. Pray for Mental Clarity and Focus:
Ask God to give you sharp thinking and wisdom to make good decisions. "For the Lord grants wisdom! From His mouth come knowledge and understanding." – Proverbs 2:6 (NLT)

4. Pray for a Renewed Mindset:
Ask God to help you see yourself as He sees you—worthy, strong, and victorious. "Let God transform you into a new person by changing the way you think." – Romans 12:2 (NLT)

A 7-Day Mental Renewal Challenge

For the next 7 days, commit to:

1. Praying daily for a renewed mind and peace.
2. Declaring scripture over your thoughts.
3. Journaling moments when you overcome negative thinking.
4. Fasting from social media and distractions that feed anxi-

ety.

5. Watch how your mindset transforms when you align with God's truth.

"You will keep in perfect peace all who trust in You, all whose thoughts are fixed on You!" – Isaiah 26:3 (NLT)

A Prayer for Mental Strength and Renewal

Father, I bring my thoughts before You today. I surrender every fear, worry, and negative thought. Your Word says in Philippians 4:6 that I should pray about everything instead of worrying. I ask You to renew my mind, strengthen my heart, and fill me with peace. When the enemy tries to attack my thoughts, remind me of Your truth. I declare that my mind is strong, my heart is at peace, and my spirit is victorious. In Yahshua's (Jesus') name, Amen.

Key Takeaways

1. The mind is the battlefield where Satan attacks men the most.
2. Even Yahshua (Jesus) was tempted in His thoughts—but overcame with prayer and scripture.
3. Science confirms that thoughts shape reality—prayer rewires the brain.
4. You must replace the enemy's lies with God's truth to break free.
5. Daily prayer renews your mind and strengthens your faith.

"Let the words of my mouth and the meditation of my heart be pleasing to You, O Lord." – Psalm 19:14 (NLT)

Chapter 8: Praying for Healing – Spiritual, Mental, and Physical Wholeness

God is Still in the Healing Business

Healing is not just something Yahshua (Jesus) did in the past—it is something He is still doing today. He heals broken bodies. He heals wounded hearts. He heals troubled minds. "I am the Lord who heals you." – Exodus 15:26 (NLT) Many men struggle with: Spiritual wounds (shame, guilt, feeling distant from God). Mental struggles (anxiety, depression, stress). Physical pain (sickness, chronic conditions, fatigue). But the good news is—God heals all of it. "O Lord my God, I cried to You for help, and You restored my health." – Psalm 30:2 (NLT)

The Three Levels of Healing

1. Spiritual Healing – Restoring Your Relationship with God:
   Many men feel spiritually disconnected from God because

of past sins or mistakes. But God does not hold your past against you. He forgives you. He restores you. He renews your spirit. "Come back to Me, and I will heal your wayward hearts." – Jeremiah 3:22 (NLT) Spiritual healing happens through: Repentance – Confessing and turning away from sin. Forgiveness – Receiving God's grace and letting go of guilt. Reconnection – Spending time in prayer and worship. "Create in me a clean heart, O God. Renew a loyal spirit within me." – Psalm 51:10 (NLT)

2. Mental Healing – Overcoming Anxiety, Stress, and Depression:

The enemy loves to attack men's minds with: Negative thoughts. Fear and doubt. Unresolved trauma. Yahshua (Jesus) understands mental pain—He experienced deep sorrow and distress before going to the cross. "He told them, 'My soul is crushed with grief to the point of death. Stay here and keep watch with me.'" – Matthew 26:38 (NLT) If you are struggling with: Depression – Pray for God's joy to fill your heart. Anxiety – Pray for God's peace to guard your mind. Trauma – Pray for God's healing touch over past wounds. "You will keep in perfect peace all who trust in You, all whose thoughts are fixed on You!" – Isaiah 26:3 (NLT) Mental healing happens through: Casting your worries onto God (1 Peter 5:7). Declaring scriptures over your mind (Romans 12:2). Focusing on things that bring peace (Philippians 4:8).

3. Physical Healing – Trusting God with Your Health:

Yahshua (Jesus) healed blind men, lepers, paralytics, and the sick—proving that He is still the Great Physician. "Yahshua (Jesus) traveled throughout the region of Galilee, teaching in the

41

synagogues and announcing the Good News about the Kingdom. And He healed every kind of disease and illness." – Matthew 4:23 (NLT) If you are dealing with sickness, pray for healing. If you are dealing with fatigue, pray for renewed strength. If you are dealing with chronic pain, pray for restoration. "He gives power to the weak and strength to the powerless." – Isaiah 40:29 (NLT) However, healing also requires action. Eat healthy, exercise, and care for your body. Get enough rest and avoid burnout. Speak life over your health instead of fear. "Don't you realize that your body is the temple of the Holy Spirit?" – 1 Corinthians 6:19 (NLT)

Faith and Healing – Praying with Boldness

Some men pray for healing, but deep down, they doubt God will answer. Yahshua (Jesus) healed people based on their faith. He always asked, "Do you believe I can do this?" Faith is the key that unlocks healing. "Yahshua (Jesus) said to the woman, 'Your faith has made you well. Go in peace. Your suffering is over.'" – Mark 5:34 (NLT)

What to Pray for Healing

1. Pray for Spiritual Healing:
   Ask God to restore your connection with Him. "The Lord is close to the brokenhearted; He rescues those whose spirits are crushed." – Psalm 34:18 (NLT)

2. Pray for Mental Peace:
   Ask God to remove stress, anxiety, and fear. "Give all your worries and cares to God, for He cares about you." – 1 Peter 5:7

(NLT)

3. Pray for Physical Strength and Healing:

Ask God to renew your body and give you strength. "He renews my strength. He guides me along right paths, bringing honor to His name." – Psalm 23:3 (NLT)

A 7-Day Healing Prayer Challenge

For the next 7 days, commit to:

1. Praying daily for healing in all areas of your life.
2. Declaring scripture over your mind, body, and spirit.
3. Fasting from things that drain your energy and peace.
4. Journaling what God reveals to you about your healing journey.

"He heals the brokenhearted and bandages their wounds." – Psalm 147:3 (NLT)

A Prayer for Complete Healing

Father, I come before You today, asking for complete healing—spiritually, mentally, and physically. I surrender every wound, every pain, and every struggle to You. Your Word says in Jeremiah 17:14, 'O Lord, if You heal me, I will be truly healed.' I believe that You are the Great Healer, and I trust in Your perfect timing. Renew my heart, restore my mind, and strengthen my body. In Yahshua's (Jesus') name, Amen.

Key Takeaways

1. God is still in the healing business today.
2. Healing happens on three levels: spiritual, mental, and physical.
3. Yashua (Jesus) healed people based on their faith—so we must pray with belief.
4. Healing requires both prayer and action.
5. Declaring scripture over your life activates God's healing power.

"The earnest prayer of a righteous person has great power and produces wonderful results." – James 5:16 (NLT)

9

Chapter 9: Praying for Protection – Covering Yourself, Your Family, and Your Home

Why Every Man Must Pray for Protection

As men, we are called to be spiritual watchmen—protecting ourselves, our families, and our homes from the attacks of the enemy. We lock our doors at night to keep intruders out. We install alarms to protect our possessions. We secure our finances to guard against loss. But how often do we pray to protect our minds, spirits, and households from spiritual attacks? "Put on all of God's armor so that you will be able to stand firm against all strategies of the devil." – Ephesians 6:11 (NLT)

The Spiritual War You Can't See

Many men think that protection only involves the physical, but the greatest battles are fought in the spiritual realm. The enemy attacks marriages with division. He attacks children with deception and confusion. He attacks men with fear, lust, pride, and doubt. But God has given us authority to fight back through prayer. "No weapon formed against you will succeed." – Isaiah 54:17 (NLT) We must pray daily for God's protection over our lives and the lives of those we love.

Covering Yourself in Prayer – Protecting Your Mind and Spirit

Satan's first attack is always on the mind—he wants to fill men with: Fear – Worrying about the future. Doubt – Questioning God's promises. Lust – Distracting from righteousness. Anger – Leading to sin and division. The only way to guard against these attacks is through prayer and the Word of God. "Take up the shield of faith to stop the fiery arrows of the devil." – Ephesians 6:16 (NLT) Daily Prayer for Personal Protection: Pray for a strong mind. Pray for spiritual discernment. Pray for self-control against temptation. "Guard your heart above all else, for it determines the course of your life." – Proverbs 4:23 (NLT)

Praying for Protection Over Your Family

As a husband and father, you are the spiritual covering for your family. You must pray over your wife's mind and emotions. You must pray over your children's future and identity. You must pray against spiritual attacks on your household. "But as for me and my family, we will serve the Lord." – Joshua 24:15 (NLT)

How to Cover Your Family in Prayer

1. Pray for Your Wife's Protection:
   Ask God to cover her physically, mentally, and emotionally.

"The Lord is faithful; He will strengthen you and guard you from the evil one." – 2 Thessalonians 3:3 (NLT)

2. Pray for Your Children's Protection:
    Ask God to shield them from harm, deception, and negative influences. "The angel of the Lord is a guard; He surrounds and defends all who fear Him." – Psalm 34:7 (NLT)

3. Pray for Your Household's Protection:
    Ask God to keep your home a place of peace, love, and safety. "Unless the Lord protects a city, guarding it with sentries will do no good." – Psalm 127:1 (NLT)

How to Protect Your Home Spiritually

Just like you secure your home physically, you must secure it spiritually. Anoint your home with oil and pray over every room. Remove anything that invites spiritual darkness (ungodly media, objects, etc.). Play worship music and declare God's presence in your house. "Wherever two or three gather together as my followers, I am there among them." – Matthew 18:20 (NLT)

A 7-Day Protection Prayer Challenge

For the next 7 days, commit to:

1. Praying daily for personal protection against spiritual attacks.
2. Praying over your wife and children every morning and night.
3. Walking through your home and praying for God's pres-

ence to dwell there.

4. Declaring scriptures of protection over your household.

"The Lord is my refuge and my fortress; my God, in Him I will trust." – Psalm 91:2 (NLT)

A Prayer for Protection Over Your Life and Family

Father, I come before You today, asking for Your divine protection. Cover my mind from fear, anxiety, and temptation. Surround my wife and children with Your presence, keeping them safe from harm. Guard our home, our finances, and our future from the enemy's plans. Your Word says in Isaiah 54:17 that no weapon formed against us shall prosper. I declare that my family is safe, my mind is strong, and my spirit is secure in You. In Yahshua's (Jesus') name, Amen.

Key Takeaways

1. Spiritual protection is just as important as physical security.
2. Satan attacks men's minds, families, and homes—but prayer is our defense.
3. You must actively cover yourself, your family, and your home in prayer.
4. Praying scriptures over your life strengthens your spiritual armor.
5. Daily protection prayers invite God's presence and favor.

"The Lord Himself watches over you! The Lord stands beside you as your protective shade." – Psalm 121:5 (NLT)

10

Chapter 10: Praying for Breakthrough – Overcoming Strongholds and Obstacles

Breaking Free from the Barriers Holding You Back

Every man faces strongholds—areas of struggle that seem impossible to overcome. Some battle addiction. Some battle doubt and fear. Some battle financial struggles. Some battle a lack of purpose and direction. But no matter how big the obstacle, God has already given us the power to overcome it. "For I can do everything through Christ, who gives me strength." – Philippians 4:13 (NLT) A breakthrough happens when we stop trying to fight in our own strength and fully surrender to God.

What is a Stronghold?

A stronghold is a deeply rooted mindset, habit, or spiritual battle that holds a person captive. It controls your thoughts and actions. It limits your spiritual growth. It keeps you from fully walking in God's purpose. But the good news is—strongholds can be broken. "For the weapons of our warfare are not of the flesh but have divine power to destroy strongholds." – 2 Corinthians 10:4 (NLT) If you struggle with addiction, God can break that chain. If you battle depression, God can restore your joy. If you feel stuck in life, God can create new opportunities.

How to Pray for Breakthrough

1. Identify the Stronghold:

You cannot defeat what you don't acknowledge. Ask yourself: What has been holding me back? What fear, sin, or habit do I struggle with? What areas of my life have I not fully surrendered to God? "Let us strip off every weight that slows us down, especially the sin that so easily trips us up." – Hebrews 12:1 (NLT)

2. Pray for God's Power to Break It:

You are not strong enough to break it alone—but God is. Declare victory over your struggle. Speak life instead of defeat. Ask God for supernatural strength. "The Spirit of the Lord is upon me, for He has anointed me to bring Good News to the poor. He has sent me to proclaim that captives will be released, that the blind will see, that the oppressed will be set free." – Luke 4:18 (NLT)

3. Fight with the Word of God:

Yahshua (Jesus) overcame Satan's temptations by using Scripture. When Satan whispers: "You'll never change." Respond with: "Anyone who belongs to Christ has become a new person." – 2 Corinthians 5:17 (NLT) When Satan says: "God has abandoned you." Respond with: "Be strong and courageous!

Do not be afraid... For the Lord your God is with you wherever you go." – Joshua 1:9 (NLT) When Satan says: "You will never succeed." Respond with: "Commit your actions to the Lord, and your plans will succeed." – Proverbs 16:3 (NLT)

What Happens When You Pray for Breakthrough?

1. Walls begin to fall like Jericho. (Joshua 6:20)
2. Chains begin to break like Paul and Silas in prison. (Acts 16:25-26)
3. Doors begin to open that no man can shut. (Revelation 3:8)
4. "The Lord Himself will fight for you. Just stay calm." – Exodus 14:14 (NLT)

When you pray for breakthrough, expect things to shift in your life.

A 7-Day Breakthrough Prayer Challenge

For the next 7 days, commit to:

1. Praying daily over the stronghold you want broken.
2. Declaring scriptures over your life.
3. Fasting from distractions that weaken your spirit.
4. Speaking victory instead of defeat.

"For God is working in you, giving you the desire and the power to do what pleases Him." – Philippians 2:13 (NLT)

A Prayer for Breakthrough and Freedom

Father, I come before You, seeking complete breakthrough in my life. Your Word says in 2 Corinthians 10:4 that You have given me divine power to destroy strongholds. Today, I surrender every struggle, fear, and obstacle to You. Break every chain that has held me back. Strengthen me to walk in freedom, victory, and boldness. I declare that I am no longer a slave to fear, sin, or doubt. I am free in Yahshua's (Jesus') name. Amen.

Key Takeaways

1. Every man faces strongholds, but God gives power to break them.
2. Breakthrough happens when we surrender and trust God's strength.
3. Scripture and prayer are the weapons to overcome the enemy's attacks.
4. Declaring victory over your struggles activates God's power.
5. Expect shifts in your life when you pray for breakthrough.

"And you will know the truth, and the truth will set you free." – John 8:32 (NLT)

Chapter 11: Praying for Wisdom – Seeking God's Guidance in Every Decision

Why Every Man Needs God's Wisdom

Every day, men face important decisions that shape their future. Who should I marry? Which career path should I take? How should I handle financial struggles? What should I do in difficult relationships? Without God's wisdom, men often make decisions based on: Emotions (Reacting instead of responding wisely). Worldly advice (Listening to culture instead of God). Fear (Choosing comfort over God's best). But when you seek God's wisdom through prayer, He guides your steps. "Seek His will in all you do, and He will show you which path to take." – Proverbs 3:6 (NLT)

Biblical Men Who Prayed for Wisdom

1. Solomon – Prayed for Wisdom Instead of Wealth:

Solomon could have asked God for riches, power, or fame—but instead, he prayed for wisdom to lead well. "Give me an understanding heart so that I can govern Your people well and know the difference between right and wrong." – 1 Kings 3:9 (NLT) God gave Solomon wisdom—and because of that, He also gave him wealth and honor. Lesson: When you seek wisdom first, God provides everything else you need.

2. Daniel – Prayed for Wisdom in a Crisis:

Daniel faced a life-or-death situation when the king demanded the meaning of his dream. Instead of panicking, Daniel prayed for wisdom—and God gave him divine insight. "That night the secret was revealed to Daniel in a vision. Then Daniel praised the God of heaven." – Daniel 2:19 (NLT) God gave Daniel wisdom, saved his life, and elevated him to power. Lesson: When you ask God for wisdom, He will reveal things beyond human understanding.

3. Yahshua (Jesus) – Prayed Before Every Major Decision:

Before Yahshua (Jesus) chose His disciples, He spent all night in prayer. "One day soon afterward Yahshua (Jesus) went up on a mountain to pray, and He prayed to God all night." – Luke 6:12 (NLT) He sought God's wisdom before making life-changing decisions. Lesson: If Yahshua (Jesus) needed to pray for wisdom, how much more do we?

How to Pray for Wisdom

1. Ask God for It Daily:

Wisdom is not a one-time request—you must pray for it consistently. "If you need wisdom, ask our generous God, and

He will give it to you." – James 1:5 (NLT) God does not withhold wisdom from those who seek Him.

2. Read and Meditate on Scripture:

The Bible is the ultimate source of wisdom. Proverbs teaches wisdom for daily life. Psalms provides wisdom for emotions and faith. Ecclesiastes warns against foolish decisions. "Your Word is a lamp to guide my feet and a light for my path." – Psalm 119:105 (NLT) The more you fill your mind with God's Word, the more wisdom you will have.

3. Surround Yourself with Wise Counsel:

A wise man seeks godly advice before making big decisions. Seek wisdom from strong Christian mentors. Surround yourself with men who walk in integrity. Be open to correction and learning. "Walk with the wise and become wise; associate with fools and get in trouble." – Proverbs 13:20 (NLT) The people you listen to will shape your decisions.

4. Trust God's Direction Over Your Own:

Many men pray for wisdom but still try to control everything themselves. True wisdom comes from trusting God's plan— even when it doesn't make sense. "Trust in the Lord with all your heart; do not depend on your own understanding." – Proverbs 3:5 (NLT) Let go of fear, doubt, and pride—trust God's wisdom.

A 7-Day Wisdom Prayer Challenge

For the next 7 days, commit to:

1. Praying for wisdom before every decision.

2. Reading one chapter of Proverbs daily.
3. Seeking godly counsel from wise men in your life.
4. Journaling insights and lessons from God.

"For wisdom is far more valuable than rubies. Nothing you desire can compare with it." – Proverbs 8:11 (NLT)

A Prayer for Wisdom and Guidance

Father, I seek Your wisdom today. Your Word says in James 1:5 that if I ask for wisdom, You will give it generously. I surrender my plans and decisions to You. Guide my steps and show me the path I should take. Surround me with wise counsel and remove any distractions or foolish influences. Give me clarity, discernment, and the ability to make choices that honor You. In Yahshua's (Jesus') name, Amen.

Key Takeaways

1. Every man needs wisdom for daily decisions.
2. Biblical men like Solomon, Daniel, and Yahshua (Jesus) prayed for wisdom before making major choices.
3. Wisdom comes from prayer, scripture, and godly counsel.
4. God freely gives wisdom to those who ask for it.
5. True wisdom requires trusting God's direction over your own.

"Fear of the Lord is the foundation of wisdom. Knowledge of the Holy One results in good judgment." – Proverbs 9:10 (NLT)

12

Chapter 12: Praying for Strength – Enduring Trials with Faith and Courage

Why Every Man Needs Spiritual Strength

Life is filled with tests and trials that will challenge your: Faith – Can you trust God when things seem impossible? Character – Will you stand firm when tempted? Endurance – Can you push forward when life feels overwhelming? Many men rely on their own strength—but eventually, every man reaches a breaking point. True strength comes from the Lord. God never intended for us to carry burdens alone. When we pray for strength, He renews us. "But those who trust in the Lord will find new strength. They will soar high on wings like eagles. They will run and not grow weary. They will walk and not faint." – Isaiah 40:31 (NLT)

The Biblical Secret to Strength – Dependence on God

The world teaches men that strength is about: Power and control. Never showing weakness. Handling everything alone. But God's strength is different—it is made perfect in weakness. "Each time He said, 'My grace is all you need. My power works best in weakness.' So now I am glad to boast about my weaknesses, so that the power of Christ can work through me." – 2 Corinthians 12:9 (NLT) When you are weak, God is strong. When you surrender, He carries you. When you pray, He renews your strength.

Biblical Men Who Prayed for Strength

1. David – Prayed for Strength in His Lowest Moments:
   David was a mighty warrior, but his greatest strength came from prayer. When he was overwhelmed, he prayed. When he was betrayed, he prayed. When he was victorious, he prayed. "The Lord is my strength and shield. I trust Him with all my heart." – Psalm 28:7 (NLT)

2. Paul – Prayed for Strength to Endure Persecution:
   Paul faced beatings, imprisonment, and hardships—but he never lost faith. He prayed for strength instead of complaining. He focused on God's power instead of his pain. He understood that trials produced endurance. "For I can do everything through Christ, who gives me strength." – Philippians 4:13 (NLT)

3. Yahshua (Jesus) – Prayed for Strength Before the Cross:
   Before facing the greatest trial of His life, Yahshua (Jesus) prayed. "He was in such agony of spirit that His sweat fell to the ground like great drops of blood." – Luke 22:44 (NLT) Even Yahshua (Jesus) needed strength from the Father. He prayed, and angels strengthened Him. His example shows that prayer

gives us the endurance to overcome.

How to Pray for Strength in Difficult Times

1. Acknowledge Your Need for God's Strength:
Admitting weakness is not failure—it's the first step to real strength. "The Lord is my rock, my fortress, and my savior; my God is my rock, in whom I find protection." – Psalm 18:2 (NLT)

2. Declare God's Promises Over Your Life:
God's Word is filled with promises of strength. Declare them over your life: "God is my refuge and strength, always ready to help in times of trouble." – Psalm 46:1 (NLT) "Be strong and courageous! Do not be afraid or discouraged. For the Lord your God is with you wherever you go." – Joshua 1:9 (NLT)

3. Lean on God When You Feel Weak:
Instead of trying to handle struggles alone, take them to God. When you are tired, ask Him for renewal. When you are discouraged, ask Him for courage. When you are struggling, ask Him for endurance. "Come to me, all of you who are weary and carry heavy burdens, and I will give you rest." – Matthew 11:28 (NLT)

A 7-Day Strength Prayer Challenge

For the next 7 days, commit to:

1. Praying daily for God's strength in every situation.
2. Declaring strength-building scriptures over your life.
3. Journaling how God strengthens you throughout the week.

4. Encouraging another man to pray for strength with you.

"The Lord gives His people strength. The Lord blesses them with peace." – Psalm 29:11 (NLT)

A Prayer for Strength and Endurance

Father, I come to You today, admitting that I cannot do this on my own. Your Word says in Isaiah 40:31 that those who trust in You will find new strength. I surrender my burdens, my worries, and my struggles to You. Strengthen my heart, mind, and body to endure the trials ahead. Fill me with Your peace, courage, and unwavering faith. I declare that I am strong in You. In Yahshua's (Jesus') name, Amen.

Key Takeaways

1. Real strength comes from depending on God, not yourself.
2. Biblical men like David, Paul, and Yahshua (Jesus) prayed for strength in hard times.
3. God's promises give you the power to endure any trial.
4. Daily prayer renews your strength and gives you courage.
5. You don't have to fight battles alone—God carries you.

"The Lord is my strength and my song; He has given me victory." – Exodus 15:2 (NLT)

13

Chapter 13: Praying for Forgiveness – Releasing Guilt, Shame, and Unforgiveness

Why Every Man Must Pray for Forgiveness

Many men carry burdens of guilt and shame that weigh them down. Past mistakes haunt them. Regret keeps them from moving forward. Unforgiveness creates bitterness in their hearts. But God never intended for men to live with the weight of guilt—His grace is available for all who seek it. "But if we confess our sins to Him, He is faithful and just to forgive us our sins and to cleanse us from all wickedness." – 1 John 1:9 (NLT) When you pray for forgiveness, God cleanses you, restores you, and sets you free.

The Power of Forgiveness in a Man's Life

1. Forgiving Yourself:

Many men struggle with self-forgiveness—they believe that their past defines them. But God does not see your past—He sees your potential. Holding onto guilt stops you from fully walking in your purpose. When God forgives you, you must also forgive yourself. "So now there is no condemnation for those who belong to Christ Yahshua (Jesus)." – Romans 8:1 (NLT) You are not who you used to be. God's grace has made you new. Release the guilt and walk in freedom.

2. Receiving God's Forgiveness:

Some men feel unworthy of God's grace—but that is a lie from the enemy. God's love is greater than your worst mistake. His mercy is available to you at all times. No sin is too big for God's forgiveness. "He has removed our sins as far from us as the east is from the west." – Psalm 103:12 (NLT) You don't have to beg for forgiveness—God gives it freely. Confess, repent, and receive His grace.

3. Forgiving Others:

Holding unforgiveness is like drinking poison and expecting the other person to suffer. Unforgiveness creates bitterness. It keeps men trapped in the past. It blocks the blessings God wants to release. "Instead, be kind to each other, tenderhearted, forgiving one another, just as God through Christ has forgiven you." – Ephesians 4:32 (NLT) Forgiving others does not mean excusing their actions—it means freeing yourself. When you forgive, you release the pain and allow God to heal your heart.

Biblical Men Who Experienced God's Forgiveness

1. David – Forgiven After a Major Fall:

David committed adultery and murder, yet God still forgave him. He repented and was restored. God did not abandon him, even after his failures. "Create in me a clean heart, O God. Renew a loyal spirit within me." – Psalm 51:10 (NLT) If God forgave David, He will forgive you.

2. Peter – Forgiven After Betraying Yahshua (Jesus):
Peter denied Jesus three times, but Yahshua (Jesus) still welcomed him back. Yahshua (Jesus) did not hold Peter's past against him. He gave him a new purpose and calling. "Then Yahshua (Jesus) said, 'Feed My sheep.'" – John 21:17 (NLT) God does not discard you because of past mistakes—He redeems you.

3. Joseph – Forgave His Brothers Who Betrayed Him:
Joseph's brothers sold him into slavery, but he still forgave them. Instead of seeking revenge, he extended grace. Because he forgave, God elevated him to power. "You intended to harm me, but God intended it all for good." – Genesis 50:20 (NLT) Forgiveness leads to divine promotion.

How to Pray for Forgiveness and Healing

1. Ask God for a Clean Heart:
Pray for God to remove guilt and shame. "Wash me clean from my guilt. Purify me from my sin." – Psalm 51:2 (NLT)

2. Confess and Let Go of Regret:
Be honest with God about your past mistakes. "Confess your sins to each other and pray for each other so that you may be healed." – James 5:16 (NLT)

3. Release Bitterness and Unforgiveness:

Ask God to help you forgive those who have hurt you. "Make allowance for each other's faults, and forgive anyone who offends you." – Colossians 3:13 (NLT)

A 7-Day Forgiveness Prayer Challenge

For the next 7 days, commit to:

1. Praying daily for forgiveness and a clean heart.
2. Letting go of guilt and self-condemnation.
3. Forgiving someone who has hurt you.
4. Declaring God's grace over your life.

"If you forgive those who sin against you, your heavenly Father will forgive you." – Matthew 6:14 (NLT)

A Prayer for Forgiveness and Freedom

Father, I come to You with a humble heart, asking for Your forgiveness. Your Word says in 1 John 1:9 that if I confess my sins, You are faithful to forgive. I release every burden of guilt, shame, and regret. Help me to forgive myself and walk in the freedom of Your grace. I also choose to forgive those who have hurt me. Fill my heart with peace, love, and healing. I declare that I am redeemed, restored, and renewed in You. In Yahshua's (Jesus') name, Amen.

Key Takeaways

1. God's forgiveness is available to every man, no matter his

past.

2. Holding onto guilt keeps you from walking in freedom.
3. Forgiving yourself is necessary for healing.
4. Forgiving others does not excuse their actions, but it frees you.
5. God redeems and restores those who seek Him.

"The Lord is compassionate and merciful, slow to get angry and filled with unfailing love." – Psalm 103:8 (NLT)

14

Chapter 14: Praying for Boldness – Walking in Confidence and Faith

Why Every Man Must Pray for Boldness

Many men struggle with fear, doubt, and hesitation when stepping into their purpose. Some are afraid of failure. Some doubt they have what it takes. Some hesitate to speak truth in a world that opposes it. But God has called men to be bold leaders, warriors, and disciples. "For God has not given us a spirit of fear and timidity, but of power, love, and self-discipline." – 2 Timothy 1:7 (NLT) You were not created to live in fear. You were not created to shrink back. God has given you boldness— activate it in prayer.

Biblical Men Who Prayed for Boldness

1. Joshua – Boldness to Lead with Strength:
   When Moses died, Joshua was afraid of the responsibility of leading Israel. God reassured him that he was not alone. He commanded him to be strong and courageous. Through

prayer and obedience, Joshua walked in boldness. "This is my command—be strong and courageous! Do not be afraid or discouraged. For the Lord your God is with you wherever you go." – Joshua 1:9 (NLT) Lesson: Boldness comes when you trust that God is with you.

2. Peter and John – Boldness to Speak the Truth:

Peter and John faced persecution for preaching the Gospel, but instead of backing down, they prayed for boldness. "And now, O Lord, hear their threats, and give us, your servants, great boldness in preaching your word." – Acts 4:29 (NLT) After they prayed, the Holy Spirit empowered them with courage. They fearlessly continued their mission. Lesson: When you pray for boldness, God strengthens you to stand firm in faith.

3. Paul – Boldness to Overcome Opposition:

Paul faced constant resistance as he spread the Gospel. Instead of retreating, he asked God for courage. Despite beatings, shipwrecks, and imprisonment, he remained fearless. "So pray that I will keep on speaking boldly for Him, as I should." – Ephesians 6:20 (NLT) Lesson: Boldness is not the absence of fear—it is moving forward despite it.

How to Pray for Boldness in Every Area of Life

1. Boldness in Faith:

Ask God to give you confidence in your spiritual walk. "So let us come boldly to the throne of our gracious God." – Hebrews 4:16 (NLT) Be unashamed of your faith. Trust God with your whole heart.

2. Boldness in Leadership:

Pray for wisdom and strength to lead your family, workplace, and community. "For the Lord will be your confidence. He will keep your foot from being caught." – Proverbs 3:26 (NLT) Lead with humility, courage, and conviction.

3. Boldness to Overcome Fear:

Fear is one of the greatest tools of the enemy—but God's power is greater. "Be strong and courageous! Do not be afraid or discouraged. For the Lord your God is with you." –Deuteronomy 31:6 (NLT) God's presence gives you the strength to push past fear.

4. Boldness to Speak Truth:

Pray for the courage to speak truth in love and stand for righteousness. "For I am not ashamed of this Good News about Christ. It is the power of God at work, saving everyone who believes." – Romans 1:16 (NLT) Being bold does not mean being rude—it means speaking with wisdom and grace.

A 7-Day Boldness Prayer Challenge

For the next 7 days, commit to:

1. Praying daily for boldness in faith, leadership, and purpose.
2. Declaring scriptures of courage over your life.
3. Stepping outside your comfort zone to share your faith.
4. Asking God to strengthen your confidence in Him.

"So be strong and courageous, all you who put your hope in the Lord!" – Psalm 31:24 (NLT)

A Prayer for Boldness and Confidence

Father, I come before You, asking for boldness in every area of my life. Your Word says in 2 Timothy 1:7 that You have not given me a spirit of fear, but of power, love, and self-discipline. Strengthen my faith, so I can walk with confidence. Give me the courage to lead, speak truth, and stand firm against fear. I declare that I am bold, fearless, and unshaken in my purpose. In Yahshua's (Jesus') name, Amen.

Key Takeaways

1. Fear is not from God—boldness is a gift from Him.
2. Biblical men like Joshua, Peter, and Paul prayed for courage and received it.
3. Boldness comes from trusting that God is always with you.
4. Praying for boldness gives you confidence in leadership, faith, and purpose.
5. True boldness is not arrogance—it is moving forward despite fear.

"The wicked run away when no one is chasing them, but the godly are as bold as lions." – Proverbs 28:1 (NLT)

15

Chapter 15: Praying for Peace – Finding Rest in God's Presence

Why Every Man Needs to Pray for Peace

In a world filled with stress, distractions, and constant pressure, many men struggle to find peace of mind and heart. Financial stress weighs heavily on men. Relationship challenges create emotional turmoil. The pressure to provide and succeed leads to anxiety. But God never designed men to carry burdens alone— He calls us to rest in His presence. "Then Yahshua (Jesus) said, 'Come to me, all of you who are weary and carry heavy burdens, and I will give you rest.'" – Matthew 11:28 (NLT) Peace comes when we surrender our worries to God. Prayer is the key to experiencing lasting peace.

What Does God's Peace Look Like?

Many men chase after temporary peace through: Entertainment (movies, sports, video games). Money and success. Avoiding problems instead of addressing them. But true peace is not found in external things—it is found in God. "You will keep in perfect peace all who trust in You, all whose thoughts are fixed on You!" – Isaiah 26:3 (NLT) God's peace is not dependent on circumstances. It is an unshakable calm that guards your heart and mind.

Biblical Men Who Found Peace Through Prayer

1. David – Peace in the Midst of Chaos:
   David faced wars, betrayal, and life-threatening situations, yet he remained at peace through prayer. "I will lie down and sleep in peace, for You alone, O Lord, will keep me safe." – Psalm 4:8 (NLT) He trusted God's protection even when surrounded by enemies.

2. Daniel – Peace in the Face of Death:
   Daniel was thrown into the lions' den, but instead of fear, he prayed and trusted God. "My God sent His angel to shut the lions' mouths so that they would not hurt me." – Daniel 6:22 (NLT) Prayer gives you peace even in life's most dangerous moments.

3. Yahshua (Jesus) – Peace in the Storm:
   When a violent storm hit while Yahshua (Jesus) and His disciples were in a boat, He remained completely at peace— because He trusted His Father. "Suddenly, a fierce storm struck the lake... But Yahshua (Jesus) was sleeping." – Matthew 8:24 (NLT) Yahshua (Jesus) was never anxious because He knew God was in control.

How to Pray for Peace in Every Situation

71

1. Give Your Worries to God:

If something steals your peace, it is a sign that you need to surrender it to God. "Don't worry about anything; instead, pray about everything. Tell God what you need, and thank Him for all He has done." – Philippians 4:6 (NLT) Worry accomplishes nothing—prayer accomplishes everything.

2. Speak Peace Over Your Life:

God has given you authority to declare peace over your mind, family, and future. "The Lord gives His people strength. The Lord blesses them with peace." – Psalm 29:11 (NLT) Speak life and reject thoughts of fear, anxiety, and stress.

3. Fix Your Mind on God's Promises:

Instead of focusing on problems, focus on God's truth. "Let the peace that comes from Christ rule in your hearts." – Colossians 3:15 (NLT) What you meditate on will shape your peace.

A 7-Day Peace Prayer Challenge

For the next 7 days, commit to:

1. Praying for peace every morning before starting your day.
2. Surrendering every worry and fear to God.
3. Reading one scripture about peace daily.
4. Speaking words of peace over your life and family.

"Now may the Lord of peace Himself give you His peace at all times and in every situation." – 2 Thessalonians 3:16 (NLT)

A Prayer for Peace and Rest

Father, I come before You, laying down every worry, fear, and burden. Your Word says in Philippians 4:7 that Your peace exceeds anything we can understand. Fill my heart and mind with Your presence. Guard my thoughts and emotions from anxiety and fear. I declare that I will not be shaken, for You are my rock and refuge. In Yahshua's (Jesus') name, Amen.

Key Takeaways

1. Peace is not the absence of problems—it is the presence of God.
2. Biblical men like David, Daniel, and Yahshua (Jesus) found peace through prayer.
3. Worry steals peace, but prayer restores it.
4. Declaring peace over your life invites God's presence.
5. Daily surrender to God leads to lasting peace.

"I am leaving you with a gift—peace of mind and heart. And the peace I give is a gift the world cannot give." – John 14:27 (NLT)

16

Chapter 16: Praying for Legacy – Leaving a Godly Impact for Generations

Why Every Man Must Pray for His Legacy

Every man leaves a legacy—but the question is: Is your legacy one of faith, strength, and wisdom? Or is it one of regret, brokenness, and missed opportunities? A godly man does not live only for himself—he builds a foundation for future generations. "Good people leave an inheritance to their grandchildren, but the sinner's wealth passes to the godly." – Proverbs 13:22 (NLT) Your legacy is not just about money—it is about the faith, character, and values you pass down.

What Does a Godly Legacy Look Like?

Many men focus on wealth and success, but true legacy is about: Raising children who walk with God. Building a marriage that reflects Christ's love. Teaching wisdom, discipline, and integrity. Serving and uplifting your community. "Their children will be successful everywhere; an entire generation of godly people will be blessed." – Psalm 112:2 (NLT) A godly man does not live selfishly—he prepares the next generation.

Biblical Men Who Left a Godly Legacy

1. Abraham – A Legacy of Faith:
God promised Abraham that his descendants would be as numerous as the stars because of his faith. "And through your descendants all the nations of the earth will be blessed—all because you have obeyed me." – Genesis 22:18 (NLT) Your obedience to God impacts generations after you.

2. David – A Legacy of Worship and Leadership:
David was not a perfect man, but he left behind a legacy of worship and devotion to God. "For when David had served God's purpose in his own generation, he died." – Acts 13:36 (NLT) Live with purpose—so that after you're gone, your impact remains.

3. Timothy's Grandmother and Mother – A Legacy of Faith Passed Down:
Timothy's spiritual foundation came from his grandmother Lois and his mother Eunice. "I remember your genuine faith, for you share the faith that first filled your grandmother Lois and your mother, Eunice." – 2 Timothy 1:5 (NLT) A man's faith influences generations to come.

How to Pray for a Lasting Legacy

1. Pray for Your Children and Future Generations:
Ask God to bless your children with wisdom, purpose, and faith. "Teach them to your children. Talk about them when you

75

are at home and when you are on the road, when you are going to bed and when you are getting up." – Deuteronomy 11:19 (NLT) Your children will follow what they see you live—not just what you say.

2. Pray for Your Influence to Be Godly:

Pray that your life, words, and actions leave an impact on those around you. "Let your good deeds shine out for all to see, so that everyone will praise your heavenly Father." – Matthew 5:16 (NLT) Your daily actions shape your legacy.

3. Pray for Wisdom in Stewardship:

A wise man builds, protects, and invests in what matters most. "Fear of the Lord is the foundation of wisdom. Knowledge of the Holy One results in good judgment." – Proverbs 9:10 (NLT) Make decisions today that will benefit your family tomorrow.

A 7-Day Legacy Prayer Challenge

For the next 7 days, commit to:

1. Praying over your children, family, and future generations.
2. Writing down the values you want to pass down.
3. Asking God for wisdom to leave a lasting impact.
4. Serving and investing in your community.

"Their children will be mighty in the land; the generation of the upright will be blessed." – Psalm 112:2 (NLT)

A Prayer for a Godly Legacy

Father, I thank You for the opportunity to leave a lasting legacy. Your Word says in Proverbs 13:22 that a good man leaves an inheritance for his children's children. Help me to lead my family in wisdom, faith, and integrity. Bless my children and future generations with Your favor and guidance. Let my actions today build a foundation for tomorrow. I declare that my legacy will glorify You and impact generations to come.In Yahshua's (Jesus') name, Amen.

Key Takeaways

1. A man's legacy is about more than wealth—it's about faith and values.
2. Biblical men like Abraham, David, and Timothy's family left lasting legacies.
3. Your daily decisions shape the future of your children and community.
4. Praying for wisdom and stewardship ensures a lasting impact.
5. God calls every man to leave behind a foundation for generations to come.

"Those who are righteous will be long remembered." – Psalm 112:6 (NLT)

Chapter 17: Praying for Consistency – Staying Rooted in Faith and Discipline

Why Every Man Must Pray for Consistency

Many men start strong in faith, prayer, and discipline—but struggle to remain consistent. Some pray for a season, then stop. Some commit to reading the Bible, but become distracted. Some set goals but fail to follow through. Yet, consistency is what leads to long-term success, spiritually and in life. "And let us not grow weary of doing good, for at the proper time we will reap a harvest if we do not give up." – Galatians 6:9 (NLT) Without consistency, you will never reach the full potential of what God has for you.

The Power of Consistency in a Man's Life

Most great men of faith were not perfect—but they were consistent. They prayed daily. They trusted God, even in difficult seasons. They remained faithful despite trials. "The godly may trip seven times, but they will get up again." – Proverbs

24:16 (NLT) God is not looking for perfection—He is looking for faithfulness.

Biblical Men Who Remained Consistent in Faith

1. Daniel – Consistent in Prayer:

Even when a law was passed making prayer illegal, Daniel remained faithful. He prayed three times a day—no matter the consequences. God rewarded his faithfulness by shutting the mouths of lions. "But when Daniel learned that the law had been signed, he went home and knelt down as usual in his upstairs room, with its windows open toward Jerusalem. He prayed three times a day, just as he had always done, giving thanks to his God." – Daniel 6:10 (NLT) Prayer must be a daily habit, not just a reaction to problems.

2. Paul – Consistent in Mission:

Paul faced beatings, imprisonment, and persecution—yet he never wavered in his mission. He preached the Gospel no matter the circumstances. His consistency led to millions of lives being changed. "But my life is worth nothing to me unless I use it for finishing the work assigned me by the Lord Yahshua (Jesus)." – Acts 20:24 (NLT) When God calls you, remain faithful, no matter the obstacles.

3. Yahshua (Jesus) – Consistent in Devotion to the Father:

Yahshua (Jesus) often withdrew to pray, showing the importance of consistency. He started His days with prayer. He sought God before making decisions. "Before daybreak the next morning, Yahshua (Jesus) got up and went out to an isolated place to pray." – Mark 1:35 (NLT) If Yahshua (Jesus) prioritized

79

consistency in prayer, how much more should we?

How to Pray for Consistency in Faith and Discipline

1. Pray for a Steadfast Spirit:
Ask God to help you stay disciplined, even when you don't feel like it. "Create in me a clean heart, O God. Renew a loyal spirit within me." – Psalm 51:10 (NLT) A steadfast spirit keeps you rooted even in tough seasons.

2. Develop Daily Spiritual Habits:
Pray at the same time every day. Read the Bible as part of your morning or night routine. Surround yourself with men who encourage consistency. "Anyone who listens to my teaching and follows it is wise, like a person who builds a house on solid rock." – Matthew 7:24 (NLT) Consistency builds a strong foundation for your life.

3. Focus on Progress, Not Perfection:
If you miss a day, don't quit—start again the next day. The goal is faithfulness, not flawlessness. "For the righteous falls seven times and rises again, but the wicked stumble in times of calamity." – Proverbs 24:16 (NLT) God honors persistence more than perfection.

A 7-Day Consistency Prayer Challenge

For the next 7 days, commit to:

1. Praying every morning and night—no matter what.
2. Reading at least one chapter of the Bible daily.

3. Journaling what God is teaching you.
4. Holding yourself accountable by telling someone your goal.

"Those who are planted in the house of the Lord shall flourish in the courts of our God." – Psalm 92:13 (NLT)

A Prayer for Consistency and Discipline

Father, I ask for the strength to remain consistent in my walk with You. Your Word says in 1 Corinthians 15:58 to be steadfast, immovable, and always abounding in Your work. Help me to pray daily, read Your Word faithfully, and stay disciplined in all areas of life. When I feel tired or distracted, remind me of my purpose. Let me be a man who finishes what I start and walks in unwavering faith. In Yahshua's (Jesus') name, Amen.

Key Takeaways

1. Consistency is what separates the successful from the stagnant.
2. Biblical men like Daniel, Paul, and Yahshua (Jesus) remained faithful in every season.
3. Daily spiritual habits build a strong foundation.
4. God does not expect perfection—He desires persistence.
5. A consistent man grows in faith, discipline, and purpose.

"So, my dear brothers and sisters, be strong and immovable. Always work enthusiastically for the Lord, for you know that nothing you do for the Lord is ever useless." – 1 Corinthians 15:58 (NLT)

Chapter 18: Praying and Fasting – Strengthening the Spirit, Weakening the Flesh

"This kind can be cast out only by prayer and fasting." – Mark 9:29 (NLT)

Personal Insight – A New Understanding of Power

In my career as a personal trainer, fasting was never part of the conversation. Nutrition was focused on fueling the body with 3–5 high-protein meals a day, counting macros, and never skipping meals. But as I grew in my walk with Christ, I realized that fasting isn't about starving the body—it's about feeding the spirit. My first three-day water fast was done with a brother in Christ. What started as a simple commitment became one of the most powerful spiritual experiences of my life. My body felt weak, but my spirit became incredibly strong. When hunger hit, I prayed. When I felt tired, I rested in God's Word. Every morning, I woke up feeling spiritually full—more energized than food had ever made me feel. Since then, fasting has become a consistent discipline. Whether it's intermittent fasting, the Daniel Fast, or extended water fasting, I've discovered that fasting deepens prayer and sharpens focus. And when my wife and I fast together, our spiritual connection becomes even more powerful. We are one flesh, and our unified fasting produces unified breakthroughs.

Why Men Must Fast and Pray

As men, we carry so much—responsibility for family, purpose, legacy, and leadership. But we cannot win spiritual battles with physical weapons. Fasting aligns us with God, silences the flesh, and strengthens the soul. Yahshua (Jesus) fasted. Moses fasted. Daniel fasted. Paul fasted. If the greatest spiritual warriors fasted, why shouldn't we? "Man shall not live by bread alone, but by every word that comes from the mouth of God." – Matthew 4:4 (NLT)

Scriptural Power of Fasting
- Yahshua (Jesus) fasted 40 days to prepare for His ministry (Matthew 4:1–2)
- Daniel fasted for 21 days and received divine visions (Daniel 10)
- Ezra fasted before a dangerous journey and God granted him protection (Ezra 8:21–23)
- Moses fasted 40 days before receiving the Ten Commandments (Exodus 34:28)
- Paul fasted before ministry decisions and appointing leaders (Acts 13:2–3)

Scientific Insight – What Fasting Does to the Body & Mind
- Autophagy: Fasting activates the body's internal healing and cellular repair system
- Clarity: Increases brain function and sharpens mental focus
- Emotional Reset: Lowers stress hormones and calms anxiety
- Spiritual Sensitivity: Slows down the body, heightens the spirit

When Should You Fast?
- When you feel spiritually dry or distant from God
- When clarity is needed for major decisions
- When battling temptation or spiritual warfare
- When praying for your marriage, family, children, or future
- When breaking strongholds, generational curses, or addictions

Types of Fasting
- Water-Only Fast: 1 to 3 days (or longer with guidance)
- Intermittent Fasting: Skip one meal and replace with prayer
- Daniel Fast: 21 days of fruits, vegetables, and water
- Partial Fast: Eliminate distractions (social media, sugar, etc.) to focus spiritually

How to Start

1. Pray before you fast. Ask God for strength, guidance, and purpose.
2. Set an intention. What are you believing God for?
3. Choose a fast. Let the Holy Spirit lead you.
4. Create a schedule. Include prayer, journaling, and Scripture reading.

5. Break the fast with prayer. Don't rush—stay in God's presence.

Sample Fasting Prayers

"Father, I surrender my flesh to strengthen my spirit. Give me discipline and vision."

"Lord, fill me with Your presence and remove anything that's not of You."

"Holy Spirit, lead me through this fast. Open my eyes to see and ears to hear."

21-Day Prayer & Fasting Challenge

- Days 1–7: Intermittent Fasting – Focus: Alignment & Peace

- Days 8–14: Daniel Fast – Focus: Breaking Strongholds & Soul Ties

- Days 15–21: Water-Only or Partial Fast – Focus: Healing, Revelation & Breakthrough

Keep a journal of what God shows you. You'll be amazed how fasting accelerates clarity and revelation.

Final Word – Discipline for Victory

Fasting is spiritual discipline. As men, we train our bodies— now it's time to train our spirits. Just like a soldier prepares for battle or an athlete trains for the game, we must fast and pray to walk in God's full authority. "Then your light will break forth like the dawn, and your healing will quickly appear." – Isaiah 58:8 (NLT) Fasting is not about starvation. It's about surrender. It's not about pain—it's about power. When you fast, you are stepping into divine sonship and drawing closer to your

Heavenly Father. And when you fast and pray—He moves.

19

Chapter 19: Bringing It All Together – Prayer, Affirmations, Journalism, and Meditation

Why Every Man Must Have a Complete Spiritual Routine

True transformation happens when a man is fully aligned—spiritually, mentally, and emotionally. Prayer connects you with God. Affirmations reshape your mindset. Journaling records your growth and breakthroughs. Meditation deepens your focus on God's presence. When you bring these together, you create a powerful daily practice that strengthens your faith and purpose. "Now may the God of peace make you holy in every way, and may your whole spirit and soul and body be kept blameless until our Lord Yahshua (Jesus) Christ comes again." – 1 Thessalonians 5:23 (NLT) Spiritual disciplines build a strong foundation for every area of life.

The Power of an Aligned Life

Many men feel lost, drained, or inconsistent because they: Only pray when they need something. Do not speak life over themselves. Do not track their spiritual journey. Do not practice stillness and focus. But when you commit to a structured spiritual routine, everything changes. Your faith strengthens. Your mindset shifts. Your purpose becomes clearer. "Physical training is good, but training for godliness is much better, promising benefits in this life and in the life to come." – 1 Timothy 4:8 (NLT) Just as a man trains his body, he must also train his spirit.

Bringing the Four Spiritual Disciplines Together

1. Prayer – The Foundation of Your Walk with God:
   Prayer is your direct communication with God. It strengthens your relationship with Him. It aligns your will with His. "Never stop praying." – 1 Thessalonians 5:17 (NLT) Start and end your day with intentional prayer.

2. Affirmations – Speaking God's Truth Over Your Life:
   Affirmations align your mind with God's Word. They rewire negative thoughts and self-doubt. They help you walk in faith and confidence. "Death and life are in the power of the tongue, and those who love it will eat its fruit." – Proverbs 18:21 (NLT) Declare positive, faith-filled affirmations daily.

3. Journalism – Recording God's Voice and Your Growth:
   Journaling allows you to reflect on what God is doing in your life. It helps you track answered prayers and spiritual progress. It provides clarity and direction. "Write down the vision and make it plain." – Habakkuk 2:2 (NLT) Journal what God reveals

to you during prayer and meditation.

4. Meditation – Quieting the Mind to Focus on God:
Meditation deepens your awareness of God's presence. It allows you to receive revelation and wisdom. It trains your mind to focus on truth. "I will meditate on Your glorious splendor and Your wonderful miracles." – Psalm 145:5 (NLT) Practice biblical meditation by focusing on scripture and God's promises.

How to Build a Powerful Morning and Evening Routine

Morning Routine:
Start with prayer—thanking God for a new day.
Speak 3-5 affirmations over your life.
Read and meditate on a Bible verse.
Write down your goals, thoughts, or what God is revealing to you.

Evening Routine:
Reflect on your day—thank God for the blessings.
Write down lessons learned and answered prayers.
Declare affirmations over your rest and future.
End in meditation, focusing on God's peace.

"Let the morning bring me word of Your unfailing love, for I have put my trust in You." – Psalm 143:8 (NLT)

A structured daily routine will transform your spiritual life.

A 7-Day Spiritual Alignment Challenge

For the next 7 days, commit to:

1. Praying every morning and night.
2. Speaking biblical affirmations over your life.
3. Journaling what God is revealing to you.
4. Meditating on God's Word daily.

"Seek first the kingdom of God and His righteousness, and all these things will be given to you as well." – Matthew 6:33 (NLT)

A Prayer for Spiritual Alignment

Father, I thank You for the gift of prayer, affirmations, journaling, and meditation. Your Word says in Philippians 4:8 to focus on things that are true, noble, and praiseworthy. Help me to stay disciplined in my spiritual walk. Let my mind be renewed, my faith be strengthened, and my purpose be clear. I declare that I will remain aligned with You, walking in faith, wisdom, and obedience. In Yahshua's (Jesus') name, Amen.

Key Takeaways

1. Spiritual transformation happens through consistency in prayer, affirmations, journaling, and meditation.
2. A structured morning and evening routine strengthens faith and discipline.
3. Biblical meditation allows men to hear God more clearly.
4. Speaking life over yourself reshapes your mindset and future.
5. Journaling records spiritual growth and answered prayers.

"Commit your actions to the Lord, and your plans will succeed."
– Proverbs 16:3 (NLT)

20

Chapter 20: The Power of Speaking Life – Transforming Your Future with Your Words

Why Every Man Must Learn to Speak Life

Every word you speak either builds or destroys. Your words shape your future. Your words impact your relationships. Your words reveal the state of your heart. God created the heavens and the earth with His Word. He spoke, and light appeared. He spoke, and life was formed. He spoke, and order replaced chaos. "In the beginning, the Word already existed. The Word was with God, and the Word was God. He existed in the beginning with God. God created everything through Him, and nothing was created except through Him." – John 1:1-3 (NLT) If God created the world with His words and we are made in His image, then our words also have the power to create and destroy. "The tongue can bring death or life; those who love to talk will reap the consequences." – Proverbs 18:21 (NLT) Speaking life brings blessings—speaking death invites destruction.

How Words Shape Your Reality

Many men underestimate the power of their words. They complain about their struggles, not realizing they are reinforcing them. They speak negatively about themselves, reinforcing low self-worth. They use words recklessly, not realizing the damage they cause. But God gave us the ability to declare truth over our lives. Your words create—choose to create wisely. "Then God said, 'Let there be light,' and there was light." – Genesis 1:3 (NLT) When you speak faith, you release God's power into your situation.

Biblical Men Who Understood the Power of Words

1. Yahshua (Jesus) – Spoke Life and Power into Every Situation:
   He calmed storms with His words. He healed the sick by speaking. He spoke with authority, and demons fled. "Then He got up and rebuked the wind and the waves, and suddenly there was a great calm." – Matthew 8:26 (NLT) Your words carry the authority of God when spoken in faith.

2. Joshua – Used Words to Lead His People to Victory:
   When Joshua led Israel, his words were full of faith, not fear. He declared victory before the battle was won. His faith-filled words strengthened his people. "But as for me and my family, we will serve the Lord." – Joshua 24:15 (NLT) What you declare over your family determines its future.

3. Ezekiel – Spoke Life Over Dead Situations:
   God told Ezekiel to prophesy over dry bones—and they came back to life. Even when situations looked hopeless, he spoke

93

life. His words aligned with God's power. "This is what the Sovereign Lord says: Look! I am going to put breath into you and make you live again!" – Ezekiel 37:5 (NLT) Never speak defeat—always speak life, even in difficult times.

How to Speak Life Over Yourself and Others

1. Speak Words of Faith, Not Fear:
   When you feel weak, declare God's strength. When you face struggles, declare victory. "For I can do everything through Christ, who gives me strength." – Philippians 4:13 (NLT) What you say out loud affects what you believe internally.

2. Speak Blessings Over Your Family:
   Declare God's favor over your children, wife, and loved ones. Pray for their future, success, and protection. "The Lord bless you and keep you; the Lord make His face shine on you and be gracious to you." – Numbers 6:24-25 (NLT) A father's words can uplift and protect his household.

3. Speak Life Over Your Purpose and Destiny:
   Declare that you are equipped, anointed, and ready for your calling. Never say, "I'm not good enough"—say, "God has called me and will equip me." "No weapon turned against you will succeed. You will silence every voice raised up to accuse you." – Isaiah 54:17 (NLT) What you affirm will manifest in your life.

A 7-Day Speaking Life Challenge

For the next 7 days, commit to:

1. Speaking only positive, faith-filled words.
2. Declaring blessings over yourself and your family.
3. Rejecting negative self-talk and doubt.
4. Praying for God to refine your speech.

"Let everything you say be good and helpful, so that your words will be an encouragement to those who hear them." – Ephesians 4:29 (NLT)

A Prayer for Speaking Life

Father, I ask for wisdom in the words I speak. Your Word says in John 1:1-3 that everything was created through Your Word. Help me to speak faith instead of fear, truth instead of doubt, and life instead of negativity. Let my words align with Your promises and shape a future filled with Your goodness. Let me declare victory over every area of my life. In Yahshua's (Jesus') name, Amen.

Key Takeaways

1. Your words create reality—speak wisely.
2. John 1 reveals that God created everything through His Word—we do the same with our words.
3. Yahshua (Jesus), Joshua, and Ezekiel used words to bring change and victory.
4. Speaking faith strengthens your mind, family, and destiny.
5. A man's words influence his future and those around him.
6. Commit to speaking life daily—your future depends on it.

"For by your words you will be justified, and by your words you will be condemned." – Matthew 12:37 (NLT)

Chapter 21: Final Reflections- A Life of Prayer, Power, and Purpose

The Journey of a Praying Man

You have reached the final pages of this book, but your journey as a praying man is just beginning. Throughout this book, we have explored the power of prayer, affirmations, journalism, and meditation—not as separate practices, but as a way of life. You have learned how to pray for yourself, your wife, your children, and your purpose. You have discovered the power of speaking life over your circumstances. You have gained wisdom on how to leave a legacy of faith for generations. And now, the question remains: Will you apply what you've learned? "But don't just listen to God's word. You must do what it says. Otherwise, you are only fooling yourselves." – James 1:22 (NLT) Knowledge without action is meaningless—prayer must become a daily habit.

The Man Who Prays Without Ceasing

A man of prayer is a man of power. He is not easily shaken by the world. He leads his home with wisdom and love. He walks in confidence, knowing God directs his steps. "Be on guard. Stand firm in the faith. Be courageous. Be strong." – 1 Corinthians 16:13 (NLT) When a man is rooted in prayer, he is unstoppable.

A Call to Action: Become a Praying Man Today

This is your invitation to rise up. If you have not been consistent in prayer—start today. If you have been hesitant to speak life—declare boldly. If you have neglected your spiritual growth—reignite your fire. "Look to the Lord and His strength; seek His face always." – 1 Chronicles 16:11 (NLT) The time is now—become the man God has called you to be.

A Final Prayer of Dedication

Father, I come before You, dedicating my life to a walk of prayer, power, and purpose. I commit to seeking You daily, leading my family with wisdom, and walking boldly in faith. Let my words speak life, my actions reflect Your love, and my heart remain steadfast in You. I declare that I am a praying man, a man of faith, and a man of destiny. Use me for Your glory, and may my life be a testimony of Your goodness. In Yahshua's (Jesus') name, Amen.

Final Words: A Challenge to Every Man

1. Do not leave this book without a plan—apply what you've learned.
2. Commit to 30 days of daily prayer and reflection.

3. Find an accountability partner to strengthen your walk.
4. Be the leader God has called you to be.

"As iron sharpens iron, so a friend sharpens a friend." – Proverbs 27:17 (NLT) Rise up and take your place—a generation of praying men is needed now more than ever.

The End... or Just the Beginning?

This concludes the book, but not your journey. Now, go forth—pray, lead, and change the world. "Seek His will in all you do, and He will show you which path to take." – Proverbs 3:6 (NLT) The Power of a Praying Man begins with YOU.

The Invitation to Salvation

A Call to Surrender Your Life to Christ

If something in this book awakened your spirit, it's not by chance—it's a divine invitation. God is calling you to Himself, and the door is open.

You can begin your journey with a simple, sincere prayer:

"Lord Yahshua (Jesus), I believe You died for my sins and rose again so I could have new life. I surrender my life to You. Come into my heart, forgive me, and lead me into Your truth. Today, I choose to follow You. Amen."

If you prayed that prayer, welcome to the family of God. Heaven rejoices with you. Now walk in your purpose and power.

Books from Kingdom Legacy Press

- The Method Man
- The Power of a Praying Man
- The Power of a Praying Athlete
- The Power of a Praying Coach
- Rooted in Goodness
- Fathers Matter

- God's Timing is Perfect Timing
- Fixing Me, Not Him
- They'll Thank You Later
- You Are Never Too Broken

Stay Connected & Grow

Visit www.KingdomLegacyPress.com to subscribe for devotionals, online studies, and upcoming book releases.

You can also find resources to help deepen your faith, strengthen your family, and live a life aligned with God.

Join the movement. Walk in purpose. Become the light.